by Mary K. Dornhoffer
and Robert F. Scherrer

Science Adviser: Terrence E. Young Jr., M.Ed., M.L.S.,
Jefferson Parish (La.) Public Schools

Content Adviser: Jan Jenner, Ph.D.

Reading Adviser: Dr. Linda D. Labbo,
Department of Reading Education, College of Education,
The University of Georgia

COMPASS POINT BOOKS
MINNEAPOLIS, MINNESOTA

FIRST REPORTS

Compass Point Books
3109 West 50th Street, #115
Minneapolis, MN 55410

Visit Compass Point Books on the Internet at *www.compasspointbooks.com*
or e-mail your request to *custserv@compasspointbooks.com*

On the cover: Gray wolf in the wild

Photographs ©: U.S. Fish and Wildlife Service/photo by Gary Kramer, cover; Art Resource, N.Y., 4;
Creatas, 5, 15, 19, 23; Image Source, 6–7; Ken Lucas/Visuals Unlimited, 8; Robert McCaw, 9, 30; Bill
Silliker Jr./The Image Finders, 10; Gallo Images/Corbis, 11; Joe McDonald/Tom Stack & Associates,
12, 18; Unicorn Stock Photos/Jack Milchanowski, 13; James Allen/Bruce Coleman Inc., 14; Gary
Milburn/Tom Stack & Associates, 16; Thomas Kitchin/Tom Stack & Associates, 17, 43; PhotoDisc,
20–21; Tom Brakefield/Bruce Coleman Inc., 22; Warren Photographic/Bruce Coleman Inc., 24–25;
Cheryl A. Ertelt, 27; Victoria Hurst/Tom Stack & Associates, 28; Unicorn Stock Photos/Robert E.
Barber, 29; Mark & Sue Werner/The Image Finders, 32; Mark & Sue Werner/The Image Finders, 33;
Richard Day/Daybreak Imagery, 34; Unicorn Stock Photos/Robert E. Barber, 36; Denver Public
Library/Western History Department, 37; North Wind Picture Archives, 38; U.S. Fish and Wildlife
Service/photo by George Gentry, 39; Photo Network/Mark Newman, 40.

Editor: Patricia Stockland
Photo Researcher: Svetlana Zhurkina
Designer/Page Production: Bradfordesign, Inc./Jaime Martens
Cartographer: XNR Productions, Inc.

Library of Congress Cataloging-in-Publication Data
Dornhoffer, Mary K.
   Wolves / by Mary K. Dornhoffer and Robert F. Scherrer.
      p. cm. — (First reports)
   Includes bibliographical references and index.
   ISBN 0-7565-0579-8
   1. Wolves—Juvenile literature. [1. Wolves.] I. Scherrer, Robert F. II. Title. III. Series.
   QL737.C22D67 2004
   599.773—dc22   2003014425

Table of Contents

*NOTE: In this book, words that are defined in the glossary are in **bold** the first time they appear in the text.*

What Is a Wolf?

You may have heard stories about the big, bad wolf. In "Little Red Riding Hood" and "The Three Little Pigs," the wolf is not very nice. Actually, wolves are strong, magnificent animals. In the wild, healthy wolves avoid humans. The wolf in "The Jungle Book" is a good wolf. Other stories, like "White Fang," also teach people good things about wolves.

Depending on what you have heard about wolves, you may think they are mean, scary animals or overgrown dogs. A wolf is really

Out set Riding Hood, so obliging and sweet,
And she met a great Wolf in the wood,
Who began most politely the maiden to greet,
as tender a voice as he could.

He asked to what house she was going, and why;
Red Riding Hood answered him all:
He said, "Give my love to your Gran; I will try
"At my earliest leisure to call."

▲ *Real wolves are a lot different from the wolf in "Little Red Riding Hood."*

▲ Wolves are majestic animals.

neither. Wolves are related to dogs. A lot of the things people like about dogs are also true for wolves. Wolves are smart and loyal, just like dogs. Wolves are also social animals. They live different lives than dogs, though. Dogs like to be with people, but wolves like to be with other wolves. They may seem like big, playful dogs, but wolves are not pets. They belong in the wild.

▲ *Dogs such as German shepherds can look very similar to wolves.*

The History of the Wolf

The wolf is a member of the dog family (canids). Wolves, dogs, cats, and other carnivores, or meat eaters, all had the same **ancestor.** This great-great-great-great grandparent lived more than 50 million years ago. An early wolf was the dire wolf. It lived among the Woolly mammoths during the last Ice Age,

▲ *A fossil of the extinct dire wolf*

▲ *The gray wolf*

about 1.6 million years ago. The dire wolf was a cousin to the gray wolf, but it was larger, slower, and probably not as smart. This may be why the dire wolf became extinct about 16,000 years ago.

Today, there are three species, or kinds, of wolves: the gray wolf (Canis lupus), the red wolf (Canis rufus), and the Ethiopian wolf (Canis simensis). The gray wolf

▲ The red wolf

appeared in Europe and Asia about 1 million years ago. It first appeared in North America about 750,000 years ago. The red wolf is smaller than the gray wolf. When the gray wolf arrived in North America, it pushed the red wolf to the south. The Ethiopian wolf is rare. It is the smallest of the three species of wolves. The Ethiopian wolf is only found in a small part of Ethiopia, a country in Africa.

▲ *An Ethiopian wolf with her pups in Bale Mountains National Park, Ethiopia*

Where Do Wolves Live?

▲ *The gray wolf is divided into five subspecies.*

Five different **geographic** groups of the gray wolf live in North America. Each is a subspecies of the gray wolf. That means wolves in each group, or subspecies, have things in common that make them different from wolves in the other groups. The different subspecies of the gray wolf are the tundra wolf (also called the Mackenzie Valley wolf or Alaskan wolf), the plains wolf, the arctic wolf, the eastern timber wolf, and the Mexican wolf. All of these wolves live in different parts of North America.

The tundra wolf lives in Alaska and western Canada and is the largest of the gray wolves. The

▲ *A tundra wolf in the Columbia Lakota Wolf Preserve in New Jersey*

plains wolf lives in the plains of the western United States and parts of Canada. The arctic wolf lives in the Arctic islands and Greenland in the far north.

▲ *The arctic wolf lives in very cold regions of Greenland and the Arctic islands.*

▲ *The timber wolf*

The eastern timber wolf lives in southeastern Canada and the northeastern United States. The Mexican wolf lives in Mexico and the southwestern United States.

▲ The Mexican wolf in its natural environment of the Southwest

What Does a Wolf Look Like?

▲ *This gray wolf's thick fur protects it during cold winters.*

Although a wolf is not a dog, it looks a lot like one.
A wolf is big and furry, with long legs and large
paws, or feet. The gray wolf can weigh as much as

▲ Wolves have broad faces, with long muzzles and yellow eyes.

175 pounds (79 kilograms). Most male gray wolves weigh about 90 pounds (41 kg), about the same size as a golden retriever. Females generally weigh less than males. Gray wolves are 26 to 38 inches (66 to 97 cm) high at the shoulder. They are 5 to 6 feet (nearly 2 meters) long from the tip of the nose to the end of the tail. The farther north a wolf lives, the bigger it usually is.

Wolves have broad faces and long muzzles, or jaws. Their eyes are golden yellow. Where a wolf lives will often determine the color of its coat. This helps the wolf blend in with its **habitat.**

▲ *A gray wolf*

▲ *Gray wolves can be several different colors.*

Most gray wolves are a gray-brown color, but they come in all shades of gray, tan, and brown. Some have black patches on their backs and sides and white patches on their chests and stomachs. Some are a solid color, such as brown or black. In the far north, gray wolves can be pure white. The red wolf is smaller than the gray wolf, weighing between 40 and 80 pounds (18 to 36 kg). It has a rusty gray-red coat.

The Wolf Family

A group of wolves living together is called a pack. This is the wolf's family. A pack can range from two to 20 wolves, but a normal pack has five to eight wolves. The leaders of the pack are the mother and father. They are called the **alpha** pair. They stay with each other for life. The alpha pair are the only wolves in the pack that have pups, or baby wolves. Brothers and

▲ *A pack's alpha pair are the only ones that have pups.*

▲ A wolf pack in winter

▲ *Members of a pack often play together.*

sisters of the alpha pair may also live in the wolf pack. They all take care of each other and any pups. The members of the pack are very close. They are very loyal to each other and often play together.

How can wolves in the pack get along so well? It is because each wolf has its own place in the pack. This is called dominance order. Some wolves are higher up in order than others. The alpha pair is at the top of the pack. The **omega** wolf is at the bottom. Each wolf knows its place in the pack. A lower wolf usually will not fight a higher wolf. The lower wolf knows it probably would not win the fight. This helps all the wolves live together peacefully.

How Do Wolves Communicate?

Although wolves cannot talk, they can still communicate with other wolves. They do this by marking their scent, touching other pack mates, making body gestures or facial expressions, growling, and howling.

Wolves do not howl at the moon, but they do howl for other reasons. Wolves howl to signal to neighboring packs and to communicate with each other. They howl so they can find each other after being separated. They howl to round up the pack for a hunt. They howl when they are alarmed. Sometimes they just howl for fun. Wolf howls are beautiful animal noises.

▲ Wolves howl to communicate with other wolves.

Wolves Are Valuable Hunters

Wolves must hunt to eat, but they are not ferocious killers. The pack hunts together as a team. Wolves do not kill for fun. They have to kill in order to live. They are not wasteful animals. They usually eat all of their prey, except for some bones and fur. When wolves do kill, they usually take the weakest animal in a herd.

▲ *Gray wolves eat a white-tailed deer.*

By removing these weaker animals, the herd grows stronger. Without wolves, some animals, like deer, could take over an area. This would destroy property and upset the **food chain.** Wolves are valuable hunters!

Hunting takes up much of the pack's time. Wolves hunt in their territory, or home range. The size of a home range depends on how much food is available, what the

▲ *Wolves are not wasteful with their prey.*

▲ *Smelling is one way wolves find prey.*

countryside is like, and whether other wolf packs are around. A small range could be 100 square miles (260 square kilometers), and a large one could be 250 square miles (650 sq km). In the north, where food is scarce, wolf territories are very large. A range could be 800 square miles (2,080 sq km). The boundaries of a territory change when the wolves need to follow their food. This may happen if they are hunting animals that migrate, such as caribou.

Wolves mostly eat animals with hooves, such as deer, moose, elk, or caribou. Wolves also eat beavers, raccoons, rodents, and even fish, fruit, and berries. Wolves locate their prey by smelling it, tracking it, or accidentally finding it. Wolves will also act as scavengers. This means they will eat the remains of animals that they did not kill.

Wolf Pups

▲ *Timber wolf pups, shown here at 8 weeks old, are born in the spring.*

Once a year, in the spring, wolf pups are born. A group of pups is called a litter. There are usually four to six pups in each litter. A short time before the pups are born, the female alpha wolf will find a safe, protected area to have her pups. This is called a den. It may be a large **hollow** in a riverbank, a space between large rocks or tree roots, a hollow log, or a small cave. The den will usually have a chamber at the end of a tunnel. The same den may be used year after year.

▲ *A mother wolf with a pup outside their den*

▲ *Wolf pups lick the jaws of an adult wolf, which makes the adult wolf regurgitate food for the pups.*

For the first few days after the pups are born, the mother wolf will not allow any other wolves into the den. She stays with the pups this whole time.

The father and other members of the pack bring food to the mother.

Wolf pups barely weigh 1 pound (.45 kg) when they are born, but they grow fast. They begin to eat meat when they are about 5 weeks old. The adults bring meat to the pups in their stomachs. The pups lick the jaws of the adults, which makes the food come back up into the adults' mouths. The pups then eat this **regurgitated** food. The pack works together to raise the pups. Wolves make very good parents!

Wolf pups are born with blue eyes. These change to yellow-gold when they are 8 to 16 weeks old. When the pups are about 8 weeks old, the mother moves them to a summer nursery. This is called a rendezvous site. These are usually near water and close to the den. The rest of the wolves in the pack continue to take care of the pups at the nursery. They bring food to them, play with them, and teach them their place in the pack. When the pups are 6 to 8 months old they begin hunting. The wolf pups live in the wolf pack until they are old enough to form their own packs.

▲ *The blue eyes of this gray wolf pup will eventually turn to yellow-gold.*

How We Almost Lost the Wolf

At one time, wolves lived almost everywhere across North America, Europe, and Asia. Many gray wolves still live in Russia and its neighboring countries, as well as in parts of the Balkans. However, the wolf was pushed out of nearly all the **contiguous** United States. It is being reintroduced in several areas. It is **extinct** in almost all of Europe except for **isolated** parts of the central and southern regions and Scandinavia. This is mostly because of people's attitudes toward wolves.

▲ *A man stands with wolf skins in Montana around 1928.*

▲ *Early settlers feared wolves.*

The early settlers in North America did not like wolves. Fear and hatred against wolves got even worse when settlers started farming. In the West, after the settlers killed nearly all the bison and elk, the wolves had to hunt what was left. This meant the wolves hunted the sheep and cattle belonging to the ranchers. The ranchers did not like this, and the United States government took an active part in killing off wolves. At one point, people were paid to kill wolves.

Protecting Wolves Today

Wolves were hunted and killed for many years. The government finally realized this was a mistake. The Endangered Species Act of 1973 was passed by the U.S. Congress to protect the wolf. It is against the law to kill wolves in the United States, except in Alaska, where they are not endangered. The government is also helping to reintroduce wolves to the wild.

The red wolf almost became extinct, so the U.S.

▲ *A U.S. Fish and Wildlife Service employee holds endangered red wolf pups.*

▲ The Mexican wolf is endangered.

Fish and Wildlife Service had all the red wolves captured in the late 1970s. There were only 17 red wolves left! After they were captured, the wolves were kept in protected areas. There they could have mates and raise babies. Fourteen of the captured red wolves became the ancestors of all the red wolves that are alive today.

In 1987, red wolves were released in the Alligator River National Wildlife Refuge in North Carolina. This was the first successful reintroduction of a large carnivore to a place where it used to live. Today, there are about 270 to 300 red wolves. Almost 220 of these wolves live in captivity.

The most endangered subspecies of the gray wolf is the Mexican wolf. To save the Mexican wolf, five wolves were captured in the late 1970s. They became the ancestors of most other Mexican wolves living today. Now there are about 250 Mexican wolves. They are slowly being released into some of the areas where they used to live. There may be about 40 Mexican wolves in the wild now.

Gray wolves from Canada have been reintroduced into Yellowstone Park and in the wild in Wyoming and Idaho. Other gray wolves have been reintroducing themselves into some of the northwestern states by migrating to other areas. A large group of about 2,500 wolves lives in Minnesota. Humans reintroduced wolves there. These wolves are spreading to Wisconsin and Michigan on their own.

Although the number of wolves is once again growing, it is important that people learn about them. The wilderness needs wolves for balance. This beautiful animal was almost lost. We are fortunate to once again enjoy wolves at home in the wild.

▲ *Wolves are an important and beautiful part of the wilderness.*

Glossary

alpha—first; the strongest in an order

ancestors—grandparents, great-grandparents, and so on

contiguous—touching or connected continuously; an unbroken chain of something

extinct—something that no longer exists; completely gone

food chain—the order of predators and prey where each animal eats the next lowest animal or plant

geographic—relating to an area or the study of Earth's surface and its land and water features

habitat—places where plants or animals live

hollow—a low part of land, such as a small valley or basin

isolated—alone or apart from others

omega—last; the weakest in an order

regurgitated—thrown up or swallowed then spit back out

Did You Know?

- Sometimes gray wolves will use the paths of sled dog teams and machines such as snowmobiles. They would rather travel on the packed snow.

- Some wolves travel more than 20 miles (32 km) a day to find food.

- Wolves will sometimes follow ravens to dead animals and then eat alongside them.

- Packs as large as 30 wolves have been found living in the wild.

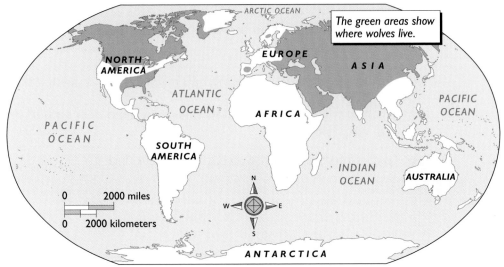

The green areas show where wolves live.

ARCTIC OCEAN

NORTH AMERICA

EUROPE

ASIA

ATLANTIC OCEAN

PACIFIC OCEAN

PACIFIC OCEAN

AFRICA

SOUTH AMERICA

INDIAN OCEAN

AUSTRALIA

0 2000 miles

0 2000 kilometers

ANTARCTICA

Range: Wolves live in Canada, Greenland, Russia and its neighboring countries, and in parts of the Balkans. The wolf was pushed out of nearly all the contiguous United States but is being reintroduced. It is extinct in almost all of Europe.

Species: There are three species of wolves and a number of subspecies.

Size: Wolves weigh 50 to 175 pounds (23 to 79 kg). Female wolves weigh 50 to 85 pounds (23 to 38 kg). Wolves are 5 to 6 feet long (1.5 to 1.8 meters) and are about 26 to 38 inches (66 to 97 centimeters) tall.

Diet: Wolves mostly eat animals with hooves, such as deer, moose, elk, or caribou. Wolves also eat beavers, raccoons, rodents, and even fish, fruit, and berries.

Young: Female wolves give birth to one to nine pups at a time. Litters average four to six pups. The pups live with their mother until they are about 5 weeks old. Then the pack raises the pups.

Want to Know More?

At the Library

Barrett, Jalma. *Wolf*. Woodbridge, Conn.: Blackbirch Press, Inc., 2000.
Harrington, Fred H. *The Gray Wolf*. New York: PowerKids Press, 2002.
London, Jack. *White Fang*. New York: Franklin Watts, 1967.
Schaefer, Lola M. *Wolves: Life in the Pack*. Mankato, Minn.:
Bridgestone Books, 2001.

On the Web

For more information on wolves, use FactHound
to track down Web sites related to this book.

1. Go to *www.compasspointbooks.com/facthound*
2. Type in this book ID: 0756505798
3. Click on the *Fetch It* button.

Your trusty FactHound will fetch the best Web sites for you!

Through the Mail

National Wildlife Federation
11100 Wildlife Center Drive
Reston, VA 20190-5362
703/438-6000
For more information about how to help wolves

On the Road

International Wolf Center
Teaching the World about Wolves
1396 Highway 169
Ely, MN 55731-8129
218/365-4695
To see captive wolves and visit one of the most inclusive centers
for wolf education and conservation

Index

About the Authors

Mary K. Dornhoffer holds a degree in chemistry and a minor in English and has been a scientific writer for the past 17 years. In addition to authoring technical manuals, scientific proposals, and children's books, she is a published poet. She lives near Little Rock, Arkansas, with her husband, John, and her two boys, Tommy and Jimmy.

Robert Scherrer's career has been in computer science and information systems. He has also pursued numerous activities based on his lifelong interest in animals. Presently, he volunteers at the St. Louis Zoo, where he does animal observation for the zoo's research group. He lives in St. Louis, Missouri, with his wife, Joan.